# EASY CELLO REPERTOIRE
## with simple piano accompaniment

# Short Cello Pieces

### Arranged by Hywel Davies

Bosworth

Exclusive distributors:
**Hal Leonard**

Order No. BOE005186
ISBN 1-84449-250-8
This book © Copyright 2004 Bosworth.

Compilation by Michael Ahmad.
Cello part edited by Zoë Thomas.
Music Engraved by Camden Music.


**www.halleonard.com**

# The Swan

## from 'The Carnival of the Animals'

Camille Saint-Saëns

# Air On A G String

from 'Suite No.3 in D minor'

Johann Sebastian Bach

**Lento, espressivo**

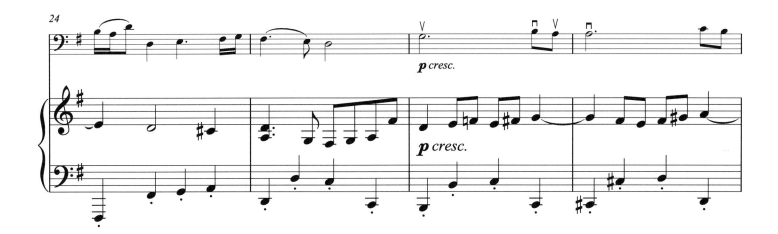

# Angels

Words & Music by Robbie Williams &
Guy Chambers

**Moderately**

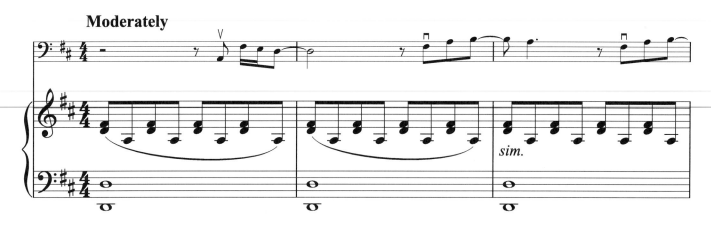

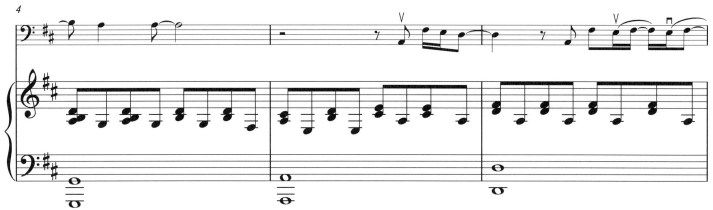

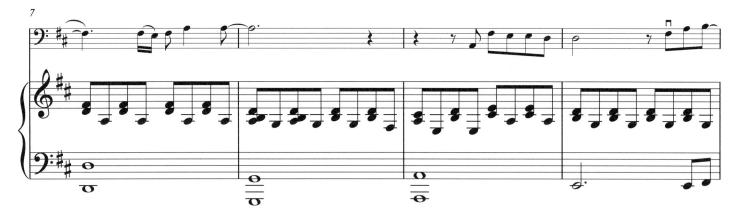

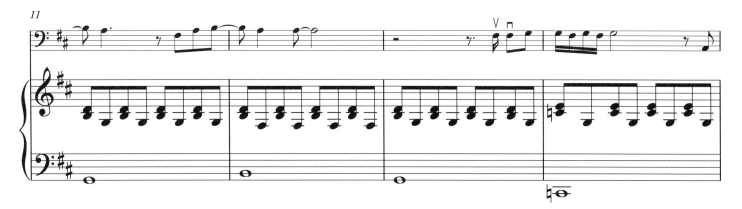

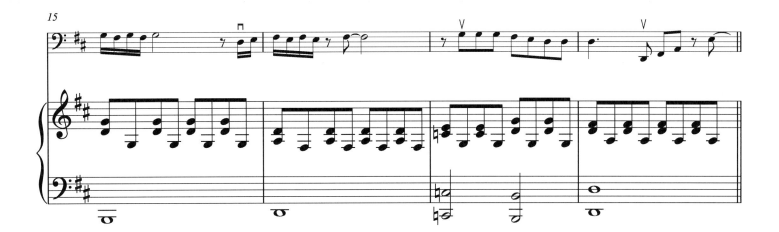

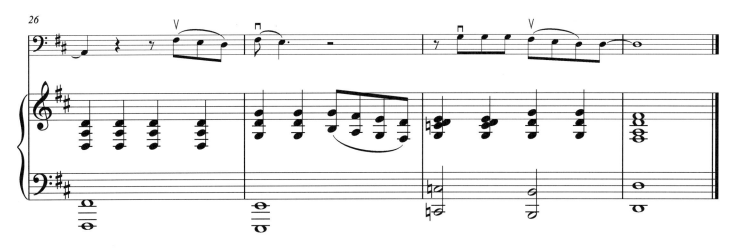

# Au Fond Du Temple Saint

from 'The Pearl Fishers'

Georges Bizet

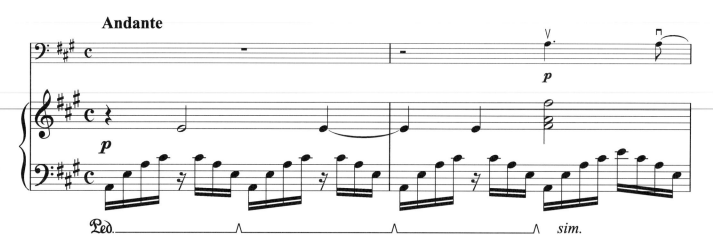

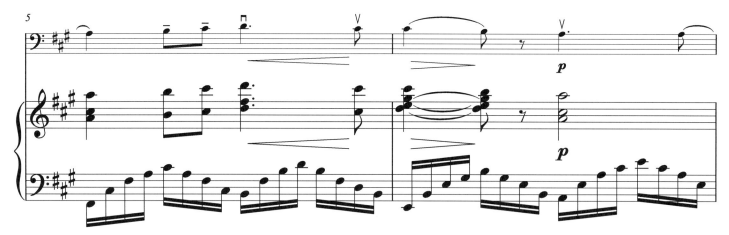

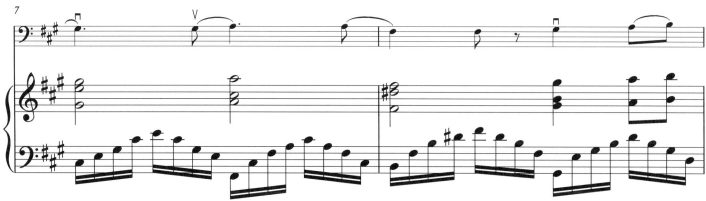

# The Ash Grove

Traditional

# Beauty & the Beast

from the musical

Words by Howard Ashman
Music by Alan Menken

**Slowly**

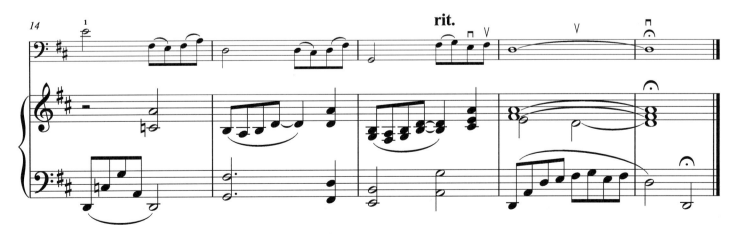

# Cello Concerto

## (1st movement, 2nd theme)

Antonín Dvořák

# Cello Concerto, Op.85

## (1st movement, main theme)

Edward Elgar

# Cry Me A River

Words & Music by Arthur Hamilton

**Slowly** ♩ = 72 (swing quavers)

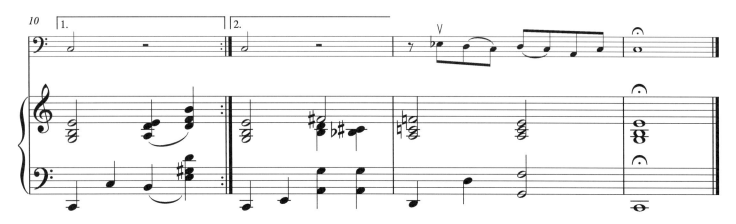

# Deck The Halls

Traditional

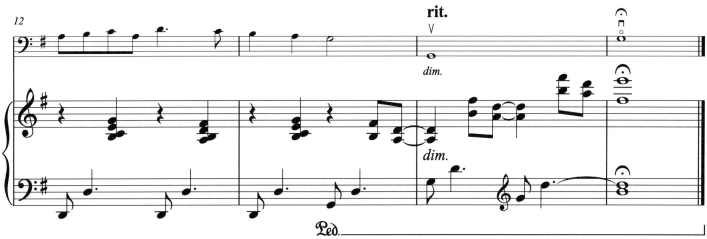

# Largo

from 'Serse'

George Frideric Handel

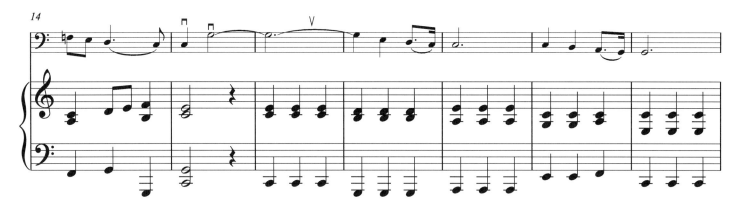

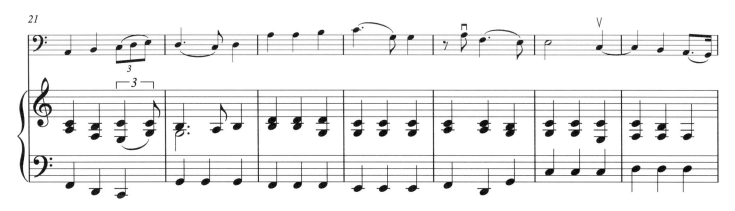

# March Of The Priests

from Act II of 'The Magic Flute'

Wolfgang Amadeus Mozart

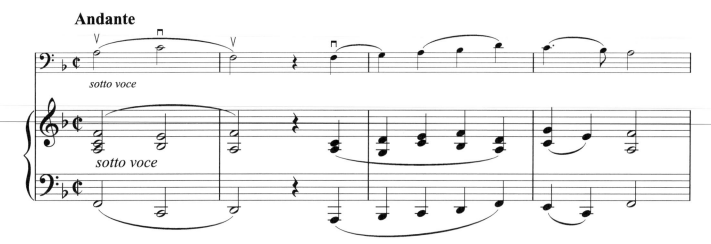

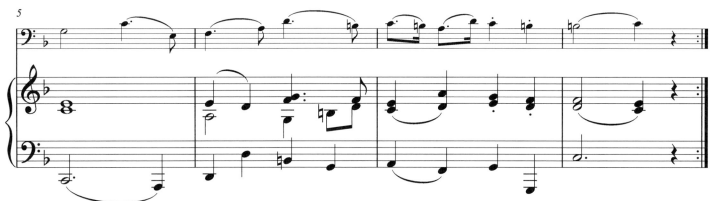

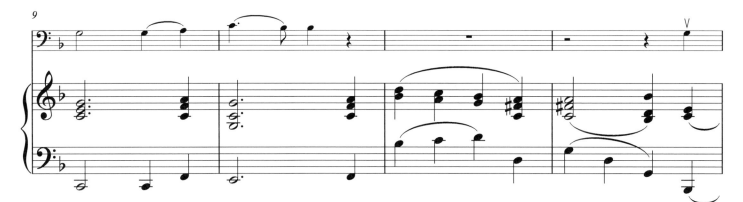

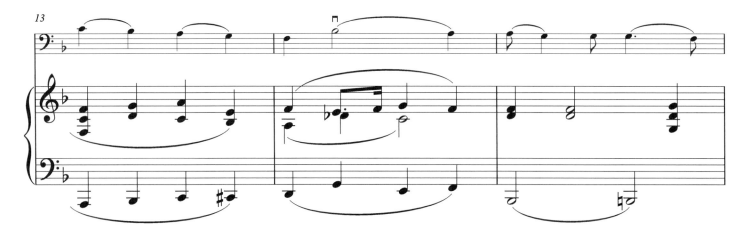

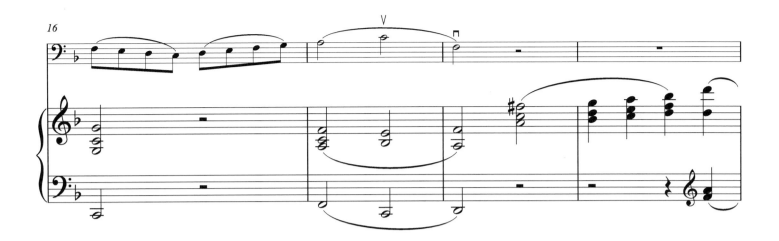

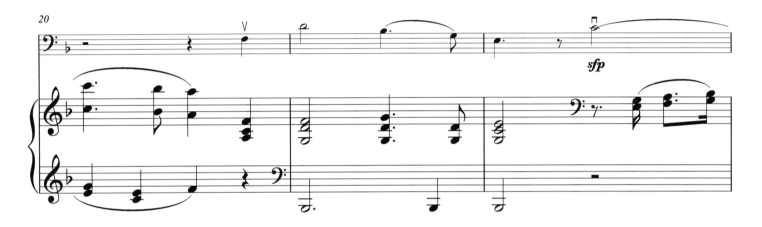

# Méditation

from 'Thaïs'

Jules Massenet

**Andante religioso**

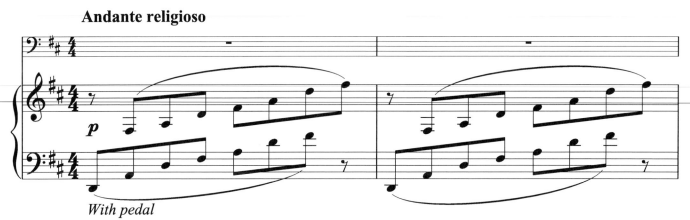

*With pedal*

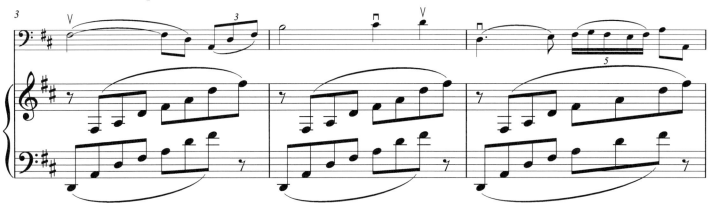

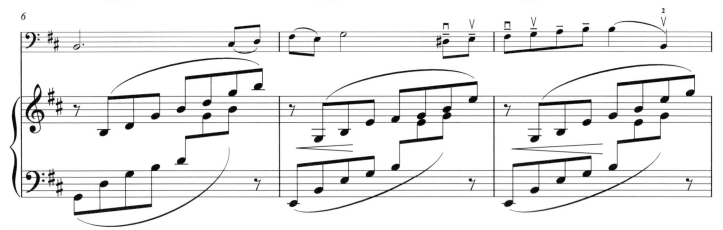

# ShortCelloPieces

Arranged by Hywel Davies

Bosworth

Compilation by Michael Ahmad.
Cello part edited by Zoë Thomas.
Music Engraved by Camden Music.
Printed in Great Britain.

# Air On A G String

from 'Suite No.3 in D minor'

Johann Sebastian Bach

# Angels

Words & Music by Robbie Williams &
Guy Chambers

**Moderately**

6

# Au Fond Du Temple Saint

from 'The Pearl Fishers'

Georges Bizet

# The Ash Grove

Traditional

# Beauty & the Beast

### from the musical

Words by Howard Ashman
Music by Alan Menken

# Cello Concerto

## (1st movement, 2nd theme)

Antonín Dvořák

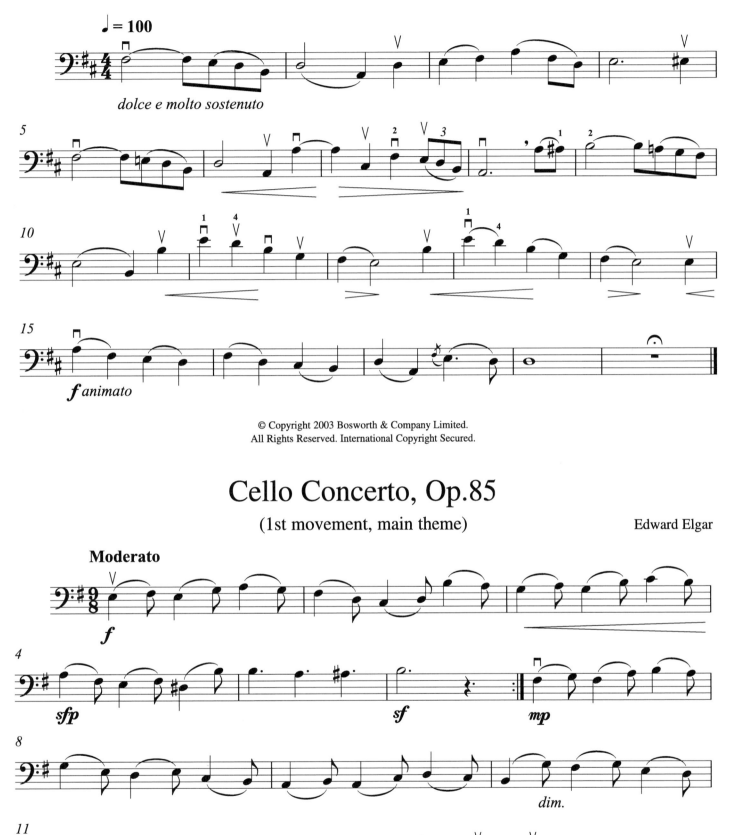

# Cello Concerto, Op.85

## (1st movement, main theme)

Edward Elgar

# Cry Me A River

Words & Music by Arthur Hamilton

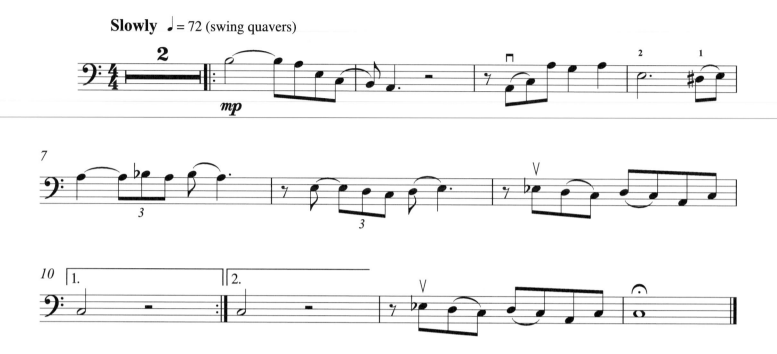

# Deck The Halls

Traditional

# Largo

from 'Serse'

George Frideric Handel

**Largo**

# March Of The Priests

from Act II of 'The Magic Flute'

Wolfgang Amadeus Mozart

# Méditation

from 'Thaïs'

Jules Massenet

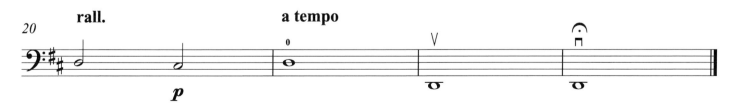

# Moon River

Words by Johnny Mercer
Music by Henry Mancini

# Memory

from the musical 'CATS'

Music by Andrew Lloyd Webber
Words by Trevor Nunn after T.S. Eliot

**Freely and expressively**

# Ode To Joy

from Symphony No.9 'Choral'

Ludwig van Beethoven

**Allegro**

15

# Raiders March

from the movie 'Raiders Of The Lost Ark'

John Williams

# Scarborough Fair

Traditional

**Moderate and flowing**

# Schindler's List

## Theme from the movie

John Williams

**Expressively**

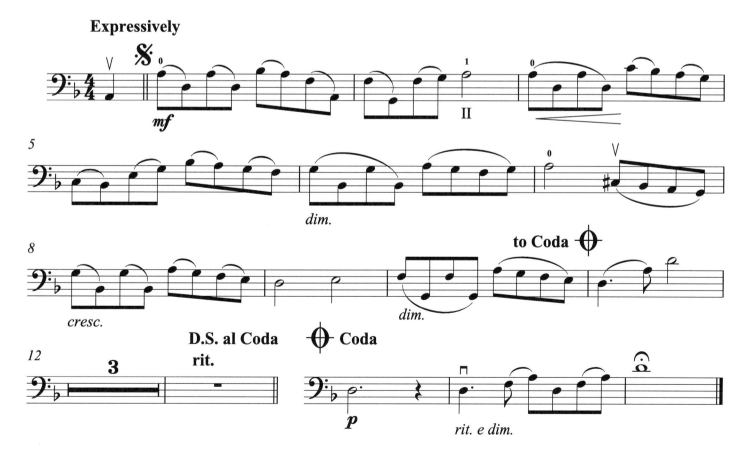

# Song Without Words, Op.19

Felix Mendelssohn

# Speak Softly Love

from the movie 'The Godfather'

Music by Nino Rota
Words by Larry Kusik

# On My Own

from the musical 'Les Misérables'

Music by Claude-Michel Schönberg
Original Lyrics by Alain Boublil & Jean-Marc Natel
English Lyrics by Herbert Kretzmer, Trevor Nunn & John Caird

19

# Träumerei

Robert Alexander Schumann

# Walking In The Air

from the animated film 'The Snowman'

Music & Lyrics by Howard Blake

# Winter Wonderland

Words by Richard Smith
Music by Felix Bernard

# What A Wonderful World

Words & Music by George Weiss &
Bob Thiele

**With a lilt** ♩. = 72

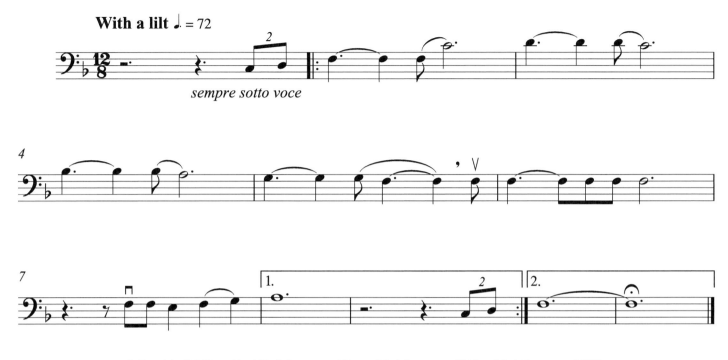

*sempre sotto voce*

# The Swan
## from 'The Carnival of the Animals'

Camille Saint-Saëns

**Andantino grazioso**

23

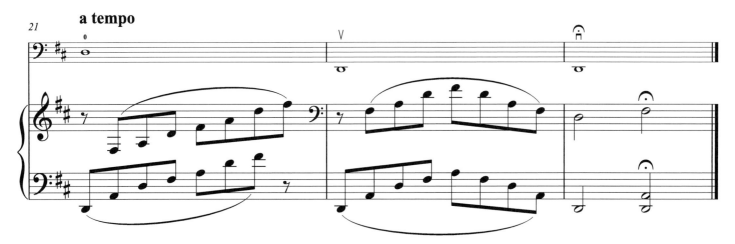

# Moon River

Words by Johnny Mercer
Music by Henry Mancini

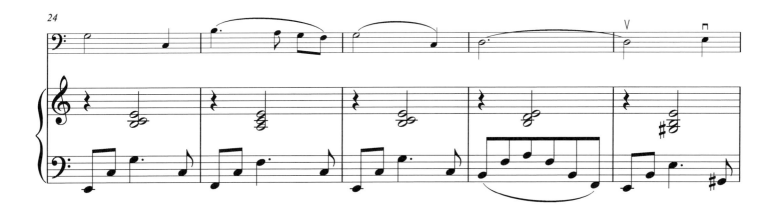

# Memory

## from the musical 'CATS'

Music by Andrew Lloyd Webber
Words by Trevor Nunn after T.S. Eliot

**Freely and expressively**

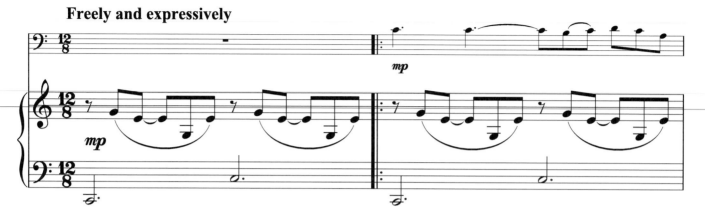

# Ode To Joy

from Symphony No.9 'Choral'

Ludwig van Beethoven

25

# Raiders March

from the movie 'Raiders Of The Lost Ark'

John Williams

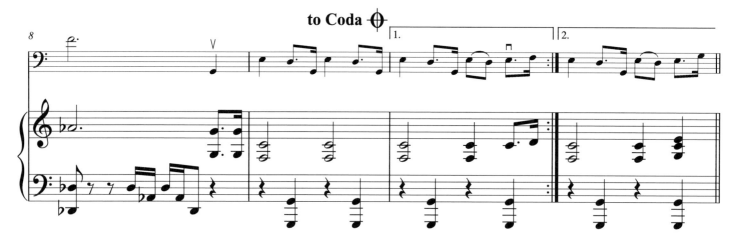

(these bars written out in cello part)

**D.S. al Coda**  $\oplus$ **Coda**

# Scarborough Fair

Traditional

**Moderate and flowing**

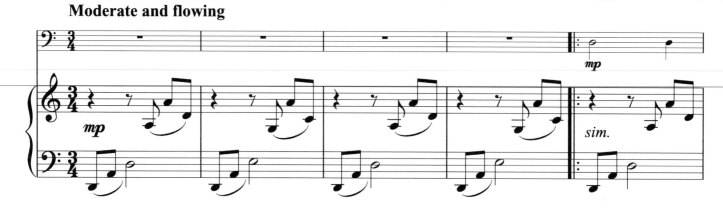

# Schindler's List

## Theme from the movie

John Williams

# Song Without Words, Op.19

Felix Mendelssohn

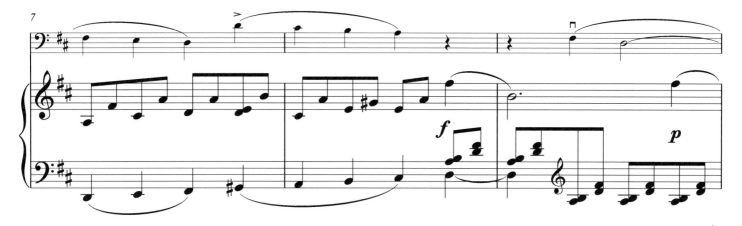

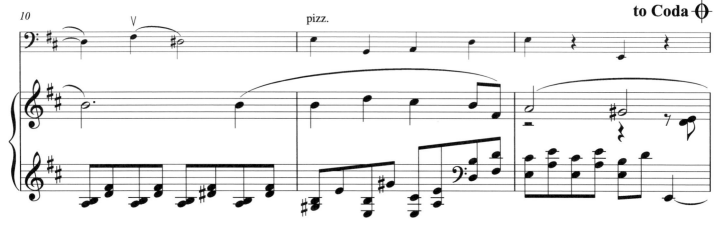

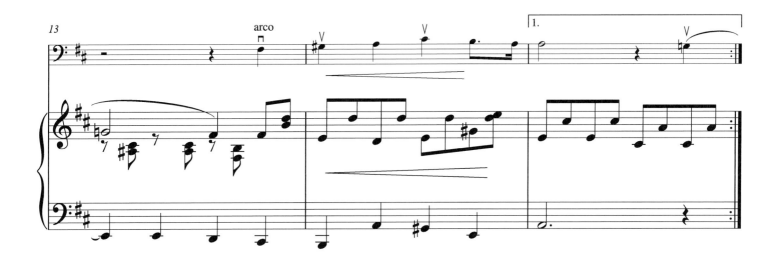

**D.S. al Coda**

**Coda**

# Speak Softly Love

from the movie 'The Godfather'

Music by Nino Rota
Words by Larry Kusik

**Slowly**

# On My Own

from the musical 'Les Misérables'

Music by Claude-Michel Schönberg
Original Lyrics by Alain Boublil & Jean-Marc Natel
English Lyrics by Herbert Kretzmer, Trevor Nunn & John Caird

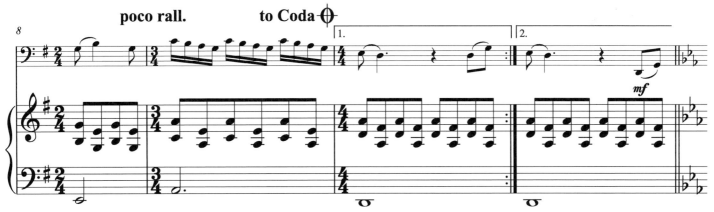

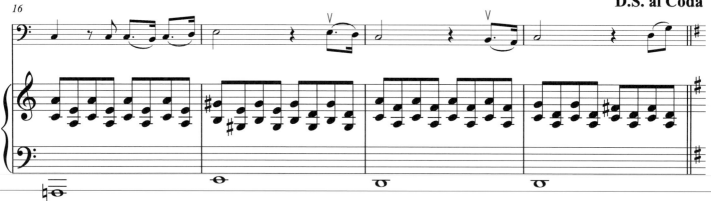

# Träumerei

Robert Alexander Schumann

# Walking In The Air

from the animated film 'The Snowman'

Music & Lyrics by Howard Blake

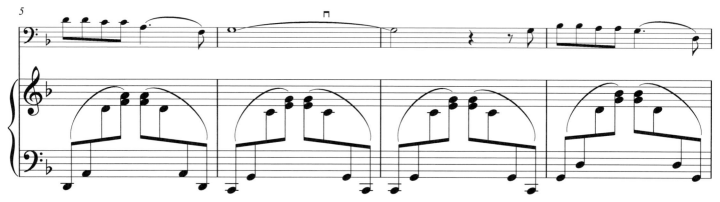

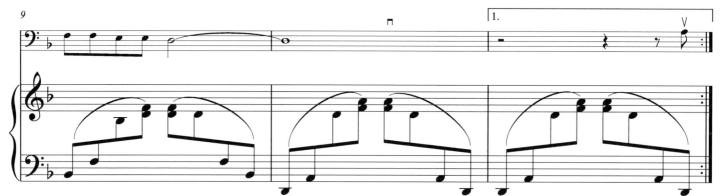

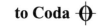

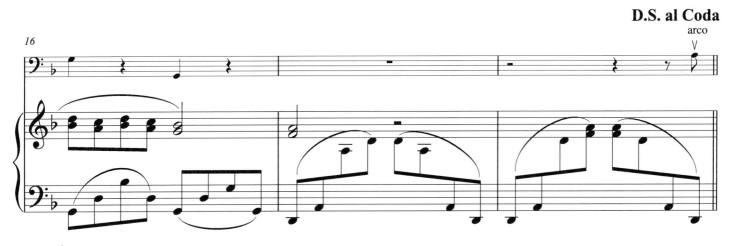

**D.S. al Coda**

 **Coda**

**Slower**

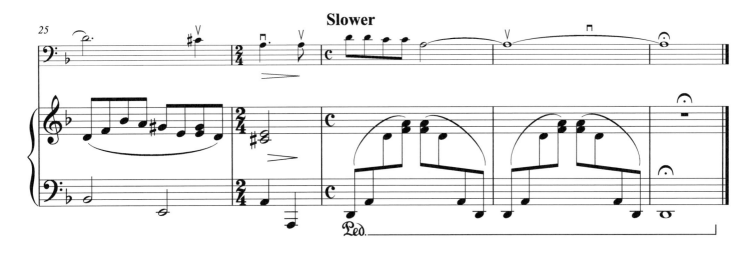

# Winter Wonderland

Words by Richard Smith
Music by Felix Bernard

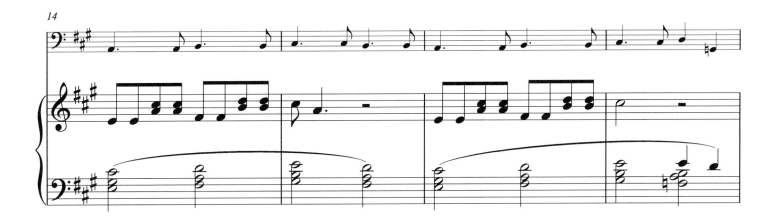

**D.S. al Coda**

**Coda**

# What A Wonderful World

Words & Music by George Weiss & Bob Thiele

**With a lilt** ♩. = 72

*sempre sotto voce*

*sempre sotto voce*